ER
Ring
Ring, Susan.

6-8-09

Polar babies /

A NOTE TO PARENTS

When your children are ready to "step into reading," giving them the right books is as crucial as giving them the right food to eat. **Step into Reading Books** present exciting stories and information reinforced with lively, colorful illustrations that make learning to read fun, satisfying, and worthwhile. They are priced so that acquiring an entire library of them is affordable. And they are beginning readers with a difference—they're written on five levels.

Early Step into Reading Books are designed for brand-new readers, with large type and only one or two lines of very simple text per page. **Step 1 Books** feature the same easy-to-read type as the Early Step into Reading Books, but with more words per page. **Step 2 Books** are both longer and slightly more difficult, while **Step 3 Books** introduce readers to paragraphs and fully developed plot lines. **Step 4 Books** offer exciting nonfiction for the increasingly independent reader.

The grade levels assigned to the five steps—preschool through kindergarten for the Early Books, preschool through grade 1 for Step 1, grades 1 through 3 for Step 2, grades 2 through 3 for Step 3, and grades 2 through 4 for Step 4—are intended only as guides. Some children move through all five steps very rapidly; others climb the steps over a period of several years. Either way, these books will help your child "step into reading" in style!

To my two little polar babies, Hollie and Jill
—S.R.

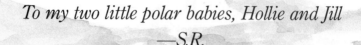

To Tyler, Peter, David, and Hunter
—L.M.

Text copyright © 2000 by Susan Ring. Illustrations copyright © 2000 by Lisa McCue. All rights reserved under International and Pan-American Copyright Conventions. Published in the United States by Random House, Inc., New York, and simultaneously in Canada by Random House of Canada Limited, Toronto.

www.randomhouse.com/kids

Library of Congress Cataloging-in-Publication Data
Ring, Susan.
Polar babies / by Susan Ring ; illustrated by Lisa McCue.
p. cm. (Step into reading. A step 1 book)
SUMMARY: Polar bear babies wake up, learn to fish, swim, walk on the ice, and enjoy running.
ISBN 0-679-89387-3 (trade). — ISBN 0-679-99387-8 (lib. bdg.)
1. Polar bear—Infancy—Juvenile literature. [1. Polar bear. 2. Bears. 3. Animals—Infancy.]
I. McCue, Lisa, ill. II. Title. III. Series. QL737.C27R55 2000 599.786'139—dc21 98-49207

Printed in the United States of America December 2000 10 9 8 7 6 5 4 3 2 1

Step into Reading®

POLAR BABIES

by Susan Ring
illustrated by Lisa McCue

A Step 1 Book

Random House 🏠 New York

Wake up,
polar babies!
It is a big day.

4

Polar babies
learn to fish.

This polar baby
loves to fish.

This polar baby
loves to sleep!

Polar babies
learn to swim.

This polar baby
loves to swim.

This polar baby
loves to sleep!

Polar babies learn
to walk on the ice.

This polar baby

loves the ice.

This polar baby
loves to sleep!

Oh, no!

A big,
big polar bear!

20

Polar babies learn
to run!

Run, polar babies!
Run!

Polar babies run
over the ice…

...past the fishing hole...

...into the water...

...and back to
their safe, safe den!

Now <u>this</u> polar baby
wants to sleep.

What does this
polar baby want?

Another big day!